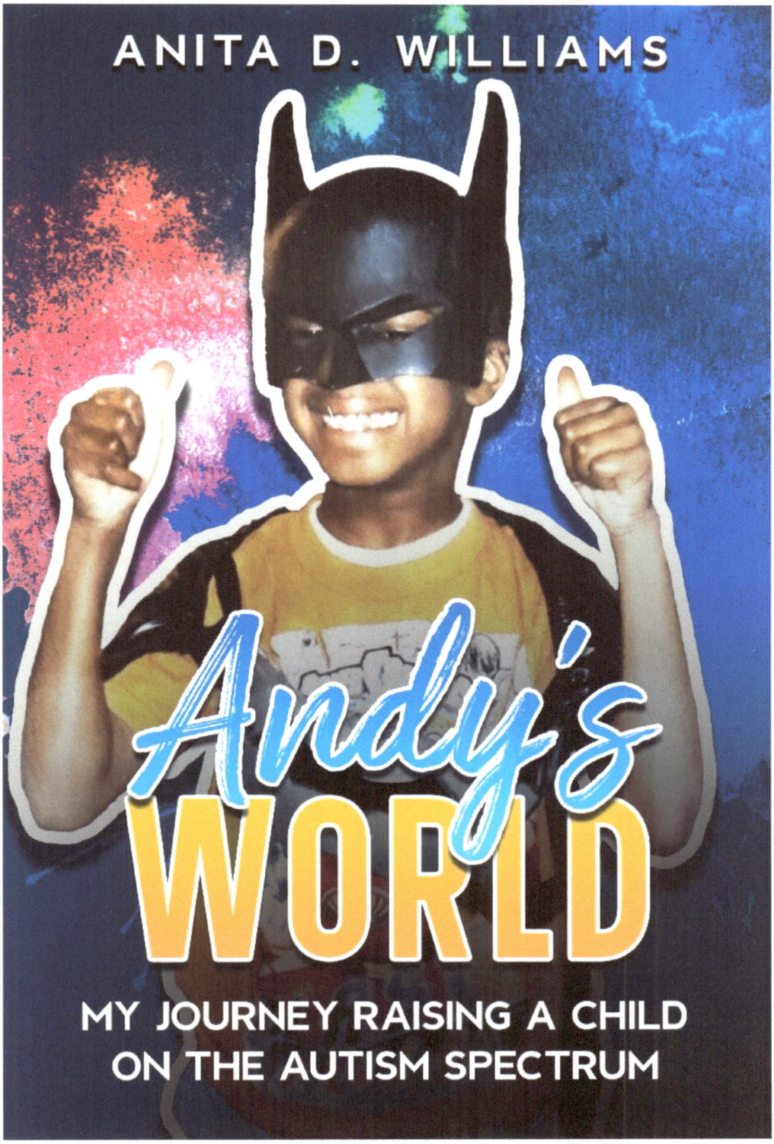

ANITA D. WILLIAMS

Andy's WORLD

MY JOURNEY RAISING A CHILD ON THE AUTISM SPECTRUM

ANDY'S WORLD

By

ANITA DIANE WILLIAMS

References/Resources

Scripture quotations marked NKJV are taken from the New King James Version®. Copyright © 1982 by Thomas Nelson. Used by permission. All rights reserved.

Scripture quotations marked MSG are taken from The Message, copyright © 1993, 2002, 2018 by Eugene H. Peterson. Used by permission of NavPress. All rights reserved. Represented by Tyndale House Publishers.

Scripture quotations marked ESV are from The ESV® Bible (The Holy Bible, English Standard Version®), © 2001 by Crossway, a publishing ministry of Good News Publishers. Used by permission. All rights reserved.

Bee chick, Ruth. (1982). A Biblical Psychology of Learning. Accent Books.

Block, Mary Ann. (2001). No more ADHD: 10 steps to help improve your child's attention & behavior without drugs! Block Books.

DEDICATION

This Book is dedicated to my beloved son,

Andersen Kevin Paul Williams

Acknowledgments

The publication of this book has been coming for a long time, and I can now share our story in hopes of encouraging others who have children on the Autism Spectrum. First and foremost, I thank **God** for the patience and tenacity in journaling as we lived our lives. We experienced some highs and many lows.

I posthumously appreciate my parents, **Nathaniel R. Rodgers and Carol Ann Demmings Rodgers**, who raised me in the fear and admonition of the Lord. My father was hands-on in raising Andersen with me. I don't know what I would have done without my Daddy.

I thank my sister, **Dr. Tamara Otey**, for always being a positive godly influence and supporter in our lives, and my brother, **Kevin Rodgers**, who helped manage Andersen on many occasions and was his buddy with the Star Wars episodes and The Marvel movies.

To my other family members, aunts, uncles, and cousins who have prayed, supported, and encouraged us on this journey.

I thank God for Andersen's grandparents, **Jerry Sr., and Diann Williams**, who have always been a source of love and encouragement.

I love my forever friends **Jolice Smith**, **Adrain Woods, Krystal Williams, and Stephanie Neckermann**, who have always been voices of reason in my life.

I also give honor to those brothers and sisters in the **Household of Faith** who agreed in prayer with me countless times for Andersen's success with the VICTORY! I won't start naming names, I don't want to forget anyone. You know who you are!

Special thanks to my birth church, **Bostick Temple Church of God In Christ, Pastor Carl and Mary Terrell,** and **Christ Community Temple Church of God In Christ**, the late **Bishop and Mother**

William Harper, the ministry where I learned how strong I was in the Lord.

To my interim church, **El Bethel Church of God In Christ, Bishop and Mrs. Nelson Watts, Jr.** my church of deliverance and a new beginning, and **Mother Rosetta Watts,** for her motherly support, **All Things are Possible Worship Center, Pastor and Minister Myrten Byrd, Jr., A Place to Worship God, Pastor Mark and Juanita Gullet**, and my home church, **Life Center International Church, Church of God In Christ, Pastor and Bishop Elijah H. Hankerson III**.

Very special thanks to **Bishop and Mrs. Edwin Bass**, who guided me through the early years by providing a preschool, "The Empowered Crayon Box."

I want to thank my coworkers **Linda Wokovich, Stacy Siebert, Karen Hayden, and Sheila Bulger,** with whom I worked, cried, laughed, and got me through some very dark days. **Linda Carol**, I love you!

I honor and thank God for sending Jesus to die and save me from my sins and for providing the Holy Spirit to empower my life with His Goodness.

~ Anita

Welcome To Holland

by Emily Perl Kingsley

I am often asked to describe the experience of raising a child with a disability – to try to help people who have not shared that unique experience to understand it, to imagine how it would feel. It's like this……

When you're going to have a baby, it's like planning a fabulous vacation trip - to Italy. You buy a bunch of guidebooks and make your wonderful plans. The Coliseum. The Michelangelo David. The gondolas in Venice. You may learn some handy phrases in Italian. It's all very exciting.

After months of eager anticipation, the day finally arrives. You pack your bags and off you go. Several hours later, the plane lands. The flight attendant comes in and says, "Welcome to Holland."

"Holland?!?" you say. "What do you mean Holland?? I signed up for Italy! I'm supposed to be in Italy. All my life I've dreamed of going to Italy."

But there's been a change in the flight plan. They've landed in Holland and there you must stay.

The important thing is that they haven't taken you to a horrible, disgusting, filthy place, full of pestilence, famine and disease. It's just a different place.

So you must go out and buy new guide books. And you must learn a whole new language. And you will meet a whole new group of people you would never have met.

It's just a different place. It's slower-paced than Italy, less flashy than Italy. But after you've been there for a while and you catch your breath, you look around.... and you begin to notice that Holland has windmills....and Holland has tulips. Holland even has Rembrandts.

But everyone you know is busy coming and going from Italy... and they're all bragging about what a wonderful time they had there. And for the rest of your life, you will say "Yes, that's where I was supposed to go. That's what I had planned."

And the pain of that will never, ever, ever, ever go away... because the loss of that dream is a very very significant loss.

But... if you spend your life mourning the fact that you didn't get to Italy, you may never be free to enjoy the very special, the very lovely things ... about Holland.

This is Andersen Kevin Paul Williams, my son
and my gift from God, and this is Andy's World!!

Andy's World is a brief look into the love, care, and understanding of why and how we were given the gift of a beautiful child from heaven.

A child reflects their parent's training …
a child left to himself brings shame to his mother…
Proverbs 29:15(NKJV).

*Point your kids in the right direction…*Proverbs 22:6 (MSG).

Some may say, "I did the best I could with what I knew." That is why we need wisdom and direction from the Word of God (Proverbs 3:5-6) guided by His Spirit. We are destroyed by not having **true** knowledge (Hosea 4:6). I want to encourage and bring cheer to parents raising children who are high-functioning on the Autistic Spectrum. I know that the spectrum has a broad bandwidth but don't ever give up on your children!

Medicine does not have the last word concerning diagnosis. Please do not misunderstand what I am saying… we need the medical field with all its gifts, knowledge, and technology in a world of sickness and disease. Physicians are earthly angels assigned by God to assist humanity. They know the human body is "fearfully and wonderfully made" (Psalm 139:14 KJV), but God has the final say!

Adventurous enough to live from his heart to take leaps of faith.

Nurturing him in the "present," whether the behavior was positive or negative.

Determined to be himself regardless of being ignored. He always said, "Mom, thanks for noticing me!" in an Eeyore tone.

Yielding to his view of the world with structure, balance, love, grace, and mercy.

Quiet Toddler

"Hey, Mommy, Chicken Little said the sky would fall." This was a typical dialogue with my 7-year-old son, Andy. The clouds were hanging low like great, big, fluffy pillows in the blue sky on this evening. "Andy, please talk about something real and not make-believe on TV." By this time of day after work, I was tired. From traffic on the highway to picking Andy up from aftercare at school to deciding what was for dinner, I was physically and mentally exhausted.

For the past few months, Andy had been in an excessively talkative state, mostly about things that were important to him. My Andy has a great imagination. That is his entire world, his imagination. To interrupt his thoughts took skillful planning.

As we walked into the local grocery store, I asked Andy to get the grocery cart. Andy's job is to push the cart. That is if he could only remember. It does not take much for my son to lose focus. You see, Andersen, affectionately known as Andy, is Autistic.

When Andy was born, I thought he was a high-needs baby. So, I tried to accommodate and soothe him as much as possible. But I was always left feeling exhausted and overwhelmed with many mental questions mixed with prayers.

At age 7, Andy underwent extensive testing due to disruptive behaviors and academic challenges at school.

I began to talk with my mother about the concerns I had regarding my son. "Mom," I said one day as we talked, "my baby's not talking." By this time, he was well over a year old and not even babbling. In fact, Andy hardly ever cried. He would smile and laugh sometimes, and his eyes were always bright with their brown-colored hue, but he was not speaking as much as most children his age.

Andy was what I called a quiet, remarkably busy toddler. He moved around the house all day like he had a job. Busy! Busy! Busy! You talk about being busy…that was our baby! And, of course, much too busy to sleep, often not even taking a nap. I have always said that God was his main babysitter because as humans, our motors ran out sooner than Andy's. Looking back, I could see the hand of God over Andy's life. He would be so busy with his toys that he never got into things that would bring him harm. *They shall bear thee up in their hands, lest thou dash thy foot against a stone.* (Psalm 91:12 KJV)

I soon began to wonder if this was coincidental or if we were just fortunate that nothing ever happened. Now I completely understand. Andy was in his own little world.

Andy never wanted to take a nap. I would have to cradle him very tight against my chest to get him asleep until he gave up the fight and fell asleep. My arms would become numb from the tightness of the hold. I did not realize at the time that he was Autistic.

Early on, I began to tune into a children's public network television station. The bright colors and moving characters in programs like "Teletubbies" were beginning to catch his attention. So I would turn on the programs that caught his attention. I never could figure out what they were saying, but Andy could. He started making the same babbling noises as the "Teletubbies." Most people said the program was silly, and all they did was baby talk.

At first, I felt embarrassed, but encouraged the program because it made Andy more verbal. I was so happy to hear "baby" talk and see him responding to something outside of himself. He even began to try to sing the songs. He was well behind other toddlers his age. I did not know what was wrong. My family and friends said, "Anita, Andy will talk when he's ready."

What I did not realize was that he could not verbally express himself. Children are supposed to know when they are hungry, thirsty, sleepy, or say "no". Not my Andy. He was too busy to tell me anything.

Andy could not correctly nurse from my breast or bottle until he was close to a year old. He was long but underweight. At ten months, I stopped the formula, put him on whole milk, and continued feeding him from the bottle for another year. My mother said, "Don't feed him in public; feed him his bottle in private because he was so big for his age." When he finally got the knack of nursing the bottle, I was happy, and he was more satisfied.

Andy's growth process was slower than others, but I kept praying, working, and caring for him at every point. My parents were instrumental in encouraging me to stay focused on Andy even when other children were ahead of him.

Then there was the Proud Parents Group. I thought it was inconsiderate of parents to brag to me about how well their children were doing and never mention the difficulties I was dealing with. Still, I would congratulate their children's successes.

The *Autism Speaks Kindness Campaign* is an initiative that encourages acceptance, understanding, and inclusion with daily acts of kindness. Andy has received more love, care, and acceptance in the past few years than ever. He still experiences people judging, misunderstanding, and treating him as if he is unintelligent before getting to know him. BEWARE!!! Andy knows and perceives more than you think.

I enrolled Andy into our local school district's *Parents as Teachers* program at two years old. This program is a global network of local affiliates who offer evidence-based home visiting programs to support healthy, safe learning, and assist children and their families to be ready to start school. This program provided voluntary in-home visits and community-based services that taught parents the skills their children needed to succeed upon entering school. It did not take long for the visiting teacher to discover some of Andy's challenges and began working with him immediately. We enrolled him in Early Childhood Special Education at the 4 years old. This was where our journey began, understanding Andy and Andy understanding himself.

Imagination

As we go through life, we naturally absorb the world around us…our specific cultures, values, trends, and norms. We add all these auto adapters to our lives. In the autism world, these adapters are shut off. Therefore, the child creates their own culture, values, trends, and norms. So often in our world, we pronounce judgment when we notice something that is not directly duplicated or seen as odd or unusual. Then we try to make it fit our mold and label it. With an autistic child, they not only break the mold, but it does not exist.

Sometimes I like his world better than mine. He doesn't always know if he's rejected, left out, or alone—the curiosity of wondering where and why things are not in place.

As other children would reach certain ages, they would continue maturing, but Andy did not because of his delayed maturity diagnosis of Pervasive Developmental Disorder (PDD). I had to learn what portions of his character, attitude, and disposition he could learn to help mature him, even if it was at a different time than his peers. This created social distance and conflict with Andy's relationships that he could not understand. He did not always know if he was rejected, left out, or alone. I knew he would not experience the details because he never knew what was happening. The details of life are needed for maturing. As we live, we should be learning and growing. When he becomes aware of an experience, he might withdraw fast and will hardly venture away from his imagination, his world.

Many do not like to admit we have an imagination or feel it is wrong to live or express ourselves from our imaginations. Our Father God, the creator of all things, has given humanity a measure of imagination/faith.

For I say, through the grace given unto me, to every man that is among you, not to think of himself more highly than he ought to think; but to think soberly, according as God hath dealt to every man the measure of faith. (Romans 12:3 KJV)

We have learned that the proper thing to do is color inside the lines, and we insist that every area of our lives be drawn in those lines. The imagination mechanism is not part of our structured lives; it is born in our spirit when we were created. If I may say, it is the part of us that is made in the image of God, the Father. Some have evil imaginations, but we are focusing on good imaginations that bring life, peace, and joy to our lives and the lives of others.

Without knowing, we sometimes purposely manipulate and control others until they lose their innate ability to imagine. This is so sad!

Andy always asks me why he must leave his imagination where he finds safety and comfort. There are times when I regret that I made him leave his imagination. He has met unlovely people, attitudes, and the ugly ways of the world. These are the experiences that take a long time for his heart to repair.

One day, I explained to Andy that I was making provisions for him to make things more normal academically. He said, Mom, "what is good about being normal."

If we could only be brave enough to be ourselves, not our desires but God's.

According as he hath chosen us in him before the foundation of the world, that we should be holy and without blame before him in love. (Ephesians 1:4 KJV).

I know this thought could take on different meanings, but my thoughts are Biblically based.

Misunderstanding the Norm

"Mom, you just don't understand" is the common statement Andy tells me. He so desperately wants to be understood in his language. Not only does everybody have their voice, but everyone has their language. They want to be understood, heard, and loved. Can two humans speak each other's language? Yes, true communication comes from lovingly listening by patient individuals.

How does one find the door to the heart? This control tower called the spirit mediates for the entire person – likes, dislikes, truths, falsehoods, character, style, personality, speech, laughter, desires, passions, sadness, and even lies. One can completely ignore this control tower (heart/spirit) and perform out of a pseudo one. Autism has created a chasm in the control room. How things in the control room are separated, aligned, and prioritized depends on the depth of the compartmentalized spectrum.

All autism on the spectrum is personalized to each specific DNA. Every human being compartmentalizes their control rooms. I have spent enough time with Andy to learn how to respect his order of compartmentalization to communicate with him and be a part of the world he has created. I had to learn to focus on Andy's behavior in order to understand the way he thinks because he was not able to express himself verbally.

My prayer request was that God show me the different sides of Andy. For example, what were autistic challenges, and what was needful correction?

Before Andy was born, I attended Bible college, where I learned a principle for child discipline from a textbook titled "A Bible Psychology of Learning." This principle has four steps that I implemented in training Andy: Teaching/Training, Instruction, Chastisement, and Rebellion.

For effective corrective behavior in the admonition of the Lord, a child must first be "taught," then given instructions on the "whys" and "how comes" of the circumstance or situation that is to be corrected. Then, if the child falls the teaching and instruction, depending on the severity of the situation, steps must be repeated.

After the first two steps have been completed and there are no signs of improvement, then the step of "chastisement" needs to take place. Chastisement is a verbal correction of the pros and cons or the level of consequences that follow a particular decision. The Bible teaches that we teach our children throughout the day (Deuteronomy 6:7-9).

Rebellion is dealt with when all the steps are arbitrarily disobeyed. Rebellion = the rod of correction. Please hear my heart! I am not advocating beating a child. When the first three steps of the principle are administered correctly, the child will very seldom have a rebellious spirit. We are all born with a rebellious spirit, but normally, a child develops a "rebellious spirit" from the atmosphere in the home. (Beechick, 1982)

Finding out that children are on the Autistic Spectrum is the beginning of knowing your children and figuring out how best to help them be successful. Children must have consistency in their lives and have parents who are proactive with their diagnoses. If parents are not together, it is better for the child to defer to the parent they spend the most time with (Mary Ann Block, 2001). This enables the child to be established in safety and security of care and understanding to help them thrive. Dissention and discord in the family will magnify the symptoms of autism and cause the child to spiral out of control. This leaves the child in a vulnerable state. Selfishness and self-centeredness in parenting are detrimental to the child's well-being.

Being on the Spectrum is not the end but the beginning of your child's personal learning experience. I have failed miserably many times in communication with Andy, especially yelling at him because I was tired or impatient. Then he guards his most cherished compartments.

When Andy is frustrated, it heightens his insecurity. I have taught him how to acclimate his feelings into the mainstream of life to be successful and survive amicably with sweetness.

The best results develop with a mix of love, respect, and appreciation with the necessary life skills and values. They all should equal understanding.

Love suffers long and is kind; love does not envy or boast; it is not arrogant or rude. It does not insist on its own way; it is not irritable or resentful; it does not rejoice at wrongdoing but rejoices with the truth. Love bears all things, believes all things, hopes all things, endures all things. (1 Corinthians 13:4-6 ESV)

This reminds me of the song by the 70s group the Bee Gees, "How Deep is Your Love?"

Sometimes, I encourage a new expedition, a new stage or as I refer to it to him as "turning the corner" for Andy for the benefit of moving forward in his life.

Of course, Andy is not interested in the future—a typical attitude of the young. Youth makes you feel as if the state of things now lasts forever. That is until you have had many birthdays that cause you to recall your life… LOL. I want to help develop everything that Heaven has awarded him. Anything new or different creates high anxiety for him, and he holds onto his normalcy like a bear with a piece of meat. I try to create a smooth transition as much as possible, which takes time. For me, it's a lesson in being more patient and receptive to his behaviors that are different from my own, leaving me anxious and frustrated. But I thank God for prayer and relying on His Word that promises to strengthen me and support me, and also a nap!

I quit my full-time job when he was 5 months old. I wanted to be with my baby. I had waited a long time for him. I knew at 18 years old that I would have trouble conceiving after being diagnosed with endometriosis, the condition that caused all my trouble every month. The doctor made a prognosis that in some years, the disease would progress, and I would need a hysterectomy before I was 30 years old. I heard what he was explaining to my mother, but my heart of hearts always heard that nothing was impossible for God (Luke 1:37). So that is where I stayed.

I conceived Andy in my late thirties and was already established in my career; therefore, according to what my mother taught me, I had time to focus on him.

After quitting my full-time job, I began working part-time for almost two years. The outcome of Parents As Teachers began with a delay in his fine motor skills, so we began working in this area. The program allowed for parental participation to assist in skills play in the home. Andy did not have a problem with this. However, he did have an issue with starting preschool away from home.

By this time, I had failed potty training. He had been wearing pull-ups and diapers at bedtime for at least a year. Andy started preschool when he was almost three years old.

Since he was starting preschool, I was returning to work full-time. It was a good thing I took off for his first week of preschool. The baby that didn't cry a lot turned into a crying baby I left with them every morning. And upon returning, he cried the same as if I were leaving him again. The daycare workers encouraged me by telling me that he would stop crying after I left, and when I returned, he'd start up again. If Andy wanted to make me feel bad, it was working!

The first week, the daycare teachers told me not to return to pick him up until three or four o'clock in the afternoon. Well, I felt like crying that whole week, just like Andy. I was very sad and worried. Now, I wasn't the mother the daycare hated to see coming (I don't think), but I knew after a while, Andy wasn't catching on in certain areas. The owner/director of the daycare was a close friend of mine. That is probably the only reason I considered letting him go. A year later, the director came to me and said she thought Andy needed special help.

So, the adventure began. Andy was tested through the area's special school district, and the results concluded that he needed help in certain areas. Unbeknownst to me, the testing revealed other challenges.

Looking back on his toddler years, I noticed that he didn't like confinement, busy restaurants, or loud music. But when he heard music, he would jump up and down and be happy. People wanted me not to let him do that at our church because it was an odd jump, but Andy was happy. People don't like things or others that are not the norm. I began to shy away from these people, including the Proud Parents Group.

By age 5, Andy was still not advancing like his classmates. Before becoming a parent, I wanted my children to attend a Christian school. In Bible college, it was emphasized that the Word of God and the regular academic curriculum were a wonderful combination. Education began with prayer, and the Bible was included in the school's curriculum. Andy was enrolled in a local private Christian school.

Once Andy started school, I was repeatedly called concerning his behavior. I was praying before, but now I had to mix prayer with faith, love, and the Word of God to get positive outcomes. Prayer, faith, love, and the Word of God are among the highest spiritual protocols you can institute into your spiritual life. It is everything for you to experience victory after victory in your life. I began to pray over him, confess the Word of God, and bind and rebuke the kingdom of darkness from further infiltrating his life. One day, the kindergarten teacher called to tell me that Andy kept jumping in front of the line. I was told this was my fault because when I prayed, I quoted the Bible scripture that Andy is the head, and not the tail!! (Deuteronomy 28:13)

Every year, every teacher explained that they did not know how Andy would be successful in the next grade. The principal at the Christian school where we had enrolled Andy called a meeting and told us they were not equipped to handle a childlike Andy. I cried, felt sorry for us, napped, and returned to my protocol… prayer, faith, the Word of God, and love. This was always my ONLY solution. (I guess by now you understand that taking a "nap" is in my protocol for success!) Nothing is impossible with God.

Anyway, conceiving Andy was a miracle within itself. My son had a purpose and destiny. The Holy Spirit always led me to people full of love, compassion, and understanding for Andy. The more of these components he had, the more he flourished. He continued to progress through every grade.

Life for us was hard, frustrating, and sometimes mundane, appearing unfruitful. Andy only ate certain textures of food and was anxious when off the beaten path or anything new. The pervasiveness of the Spectrum he was diagnosed with would drain me completely. Autism became our norm.

Andy's behavior was completely off the chain as we approached second grade. Our home was out of order, and a divorce was looming. Children can feel it when their parents are not in sync. There was a wave of uncertainty in our home. And Andy's behavior had spun out of control.

So why would I not allow Andy to express his autistic tendencies as he was born? I had some real soul (heart) searching to do. I desperately wanted him to be "normal"! I wanted God to heal him! Why was I so embarrassed? Andy was not!

I vividly remember when Andy decided to go out for the basketball team in junior high school. I was so afraid for him. Academically and socially, things were already "red-flagged." Every year, every teacher proclaimed that Andy would not be able to progress to the next level. The forecast was always dark and gloomy, with thunderstorms and rain ahead.

One year, when finances were tight, I talked with the autism education teacher about placing Andy in a public school. I was giving up. Maybe I was just tired of the new normal and exhausted by the adolescence stage he was in and the financial struggle. The fight to make passing grades was arduous, but we continued.

The teachers at the public high school explained to Andy that attending this high school would not be hard. Their curriculum afforded learning times early in the day, but by afternoon, students played on their tablets. I immediately pronounced that this was unacceptable for Andy! I had researched and studied his diagnosis. I learned that this diagnosis could learn and be educated in any subject matter, but the process would be different. So, not fully engaging his learning capacity was out of the question. The autism educator patted me on the back and said, "That's because you're a good Mama!" The public school was not going to assert Andy beyond his capacity. He would only learn what they assumed his diagnosis was capable of. Wow, here we were at another roadblock! I again found myself back at the budget board. I took another step of faith out further from the shore.

At this point, I would either believe God or go under. As I looked back, by faith, I was way out at sea, trusting God's promises. I continued to trust Him. I paid all the necessary fees for Andy to try out for the basketball team. A few weeks later, I received a call that Andy had been hurt and could not walk. My Dad brought him to my job, and I x-rayed him. Sure enough… a broken foot. He was a part of the team but could not play. Toward the end of the season, after his foot had healed, Andy got a chance to play as a team member. He showed great sportsmanship. I was impressed. I give most of the credit to their junior varsity coach. He believed in Andy, but most importantly, Andy believed in himself. At the most challenging times, he always declared that he "loved being Andy"!

Even so-called Christians who proclaimed the love of God for all treated us like "Oh, no!" or no grace allowed here, only human perfection.

Then I began to think…what was wrong with me? Why did I care that he was himself and his autistic behavior was fully visible? Notice that I didn't use the word "different". In his rare form, he was himself, and I just needed to accept it. I believed in God for complete wholeness for my son. Hmmm! I needed to believe God to end my embarrassment of my autistic child. Andy was handling himself by faith better than I was!

Andy played on the basketball team from the tenth through twelfth grade, his senior year. I learned much about this human being who God has placed in my life. At this juncture, I not only needed to evaluate my heart, but I also needed to reevaluate my faith and my belief system. I saw how many of my prayers were answered according to the things that needed alignment with the will of God for Andy's life. But to try and recreate his core, the very existence of his being, was wrong. I was tampering with creation. Andy repeatedly tells me, "Mom, you don't understand." I have always prayed for his understanding to be enlightened, but maybe my understanding needed to be enlightened to the calling that Father God planned for him, too! I needed to remember that God called Andy into life before He created the world (Ephesians 1:4-6).

My father always reminded me to deal with Andy right where he was mentally and emotionally. Most importantly, I was to watch what I said to him, be patient, and pray. And then my father would say, "please don't make him something he is not." But I would say, "Daddy, I'm trying to get him to another level!" Then Daddy said, "God knows how to deal with Andy on any level, that's not up to you!"

Train up a child in the way he (or they) should go… *and God will work out the rest of Andy's life.* (Proverbs 22:6).

Throughout most of Andy's childhood, I raised Andy as a single divorced mother. This caused Andy anxiety because of the unwillingness of the court to consider his diagnosis. Therefore, he was out of control; emotionally and mentally, plus autism, we had some real problems. What kept us grounded was family, especially my Dad and extended church family, who cared for us and helped pray for us through many turbulent days. Andy did not understand what divorce was and how our family's dynamics had changed, which set him back. We had counseling that helped us tremendously to navigate our lives. Still, Andy began wetting the bed at night and had times of uncontrolled crying and anger. He did not understand why he could not just stay at home.

Heartbroken myself, I turned to much prayer for our survival.

My story of Teddy and his six friends helped.

Teddy and His Six Friends

Teddy and his six friends—rabbit, fox, turtle, donkey, polar bear, and beaver—had been friends since they were babies growing up in the woods. Teddy's friends tried to help Teddy because his mommy and daddy had decided to live in different places. Teddy was so heartbroken. What was he going to do? He needed a plan to fix things. Teddy and his six friends had been together forever. The forest was their home.

But now Teddy's daddy wanted to go live in the mountains. Teddy knew nothing about the mountains, and he was afraid.

He had to choose Mommy in the forest or Daddy in the mountains. Now, when all the six friends gathered to help Teddy with advice, something had happened.

Teddy came running in all his excitement. "Hey guys, I learned today that I don't have to choose my mommy or daddy. Daddy said that home in the forest was the best place for me and that I could visit the mountains anytime, and he would come to the forest and visit with me. My home in the forest is the best place for me," Teddy said, leaping up and down. Teddy and his six friends were all so very happy. Now Teddy didn't have to choose. Teddy loved his mommy and daddy very much, but he loved his home in the forest best.

A Note to Parents

When parents separate or divorce, children feel they must choose mommy or daddy. The parents should evaluate both environments and decide which one the child(ren) will be able to thrive in. For emotional, mental, and spiritual stability, the best accommodation for a child is vital to their well-being, whether in the forest or the mountains. Two people may not choose to continue the relationship, but the love for their child should be the same and never change. A child should never feel the absence of love or be without a home. A child should always have a home filled with the love of God and the love of their parents, together or apart.

After a few years, our lives began to settle in our family. Andy and my Dad's relationship (whom Andy affectionately calls "Papa") continued progressing. As Andy approached high school graduation, he was on the "Honor Roll"!!! Andy enrolled in community college and has an associate degree in liberal arts. He will continue at a university of his choice. Andy has "peace" that continues to heal him from the past, allowing Andy to be the man he is today: loving, caring, kind, and happy!

ABOUT THE AUTHOR

Born and raised in St Louis, Missouri, Anita Diane
Williams is a healthcare imaging professional and
Bible scholar. She graduated from Washington
University School of Radiologic Technology
Mallinckrodt Institute of Radiology. With over 40
years of experience in Radiologic Technology, she
performs all diagnostic procedures and has spent
most of her career in Orthopedic Surgery and Sports
Medicine.

God gifted Anita with the ability to teach the Bible
as a teenager. She teaches in Sunday School,
Vacation Bible School, and various other teaching
entities in the church. She is licensed as an
Evangelist Missionary through the Church of God
In Christ, Inc. Anita is working on her second
Bachelor of Arts in Biblical Literature at Oral
Roberts University.

www.northmemphispublishinghouse.com

northmemphispublishinghouse@gmail.com

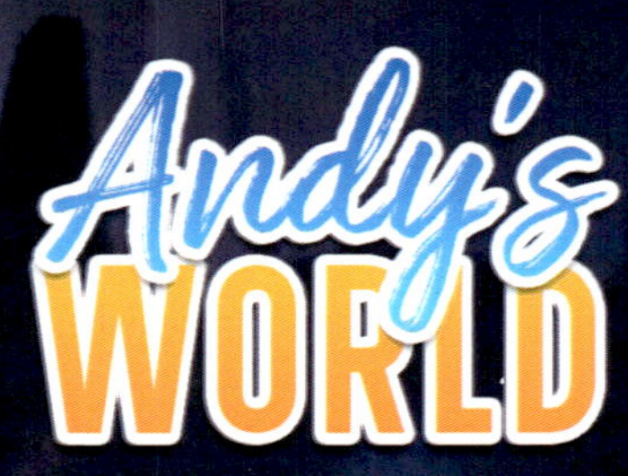

I am honored at this time to share the story of the journey of raising my son on the Autistic Spectrum. In that journey we experienced a tragic season in our lives that caused me to abandon everything and began a journey of faith seeking God with him (Jeremiah 29:11-14). Our lives have grown full circle and we have found a place of peace and grace in God relishing in His love. Enjoy! Anita.

Extemporaneous
Automatics
Jim Ivy